World Book's Learning Ladders

My Body

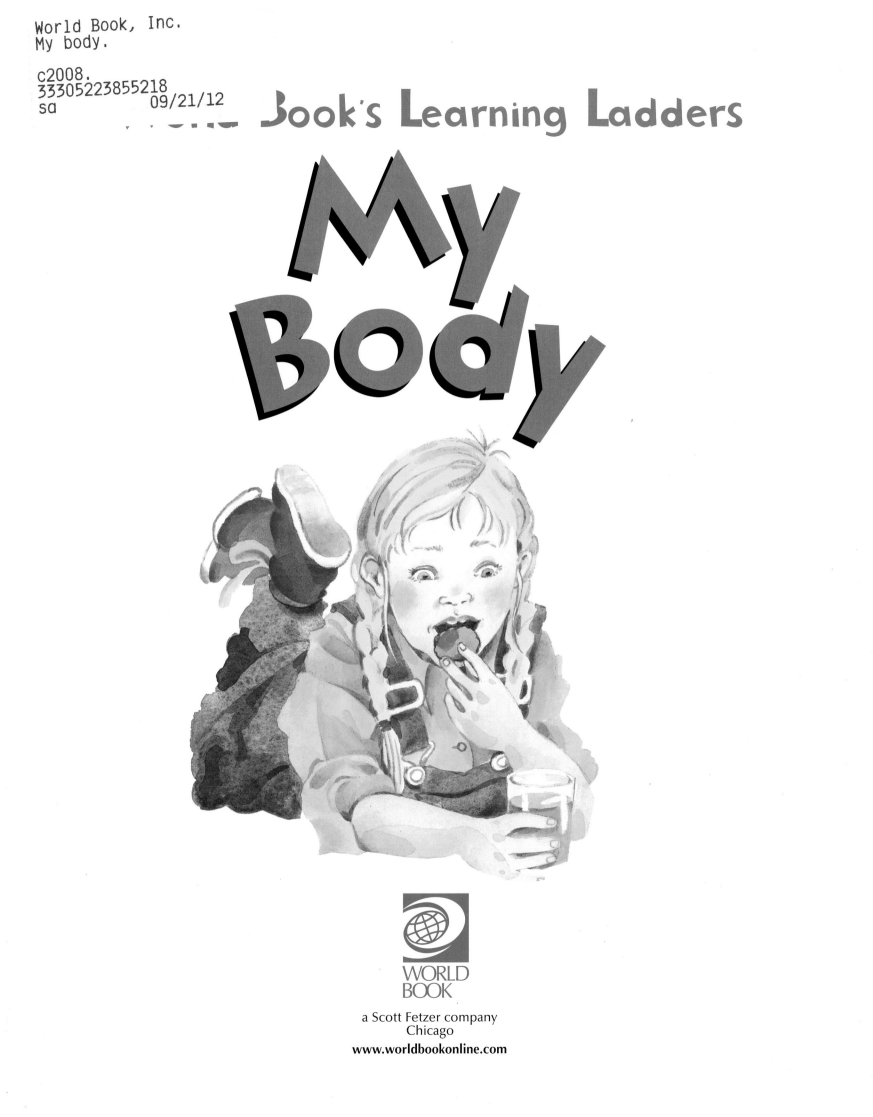

WORLD
BOOK

a Scott Fetzer company
Chicago
www.worldbookonline.com

WORLD BOOK

233 N. Michigan Avenue
Chicago, IL 60601
U.S.A.

For information about other World Book publications, visit our Web site at
http://www.worldbookonline.com or call **1-800-WORLDBK (967-5325)**.

For information about sales to schools and libraries, call **1-800-975-3250 (United States);**
1-800-837-5365 (Canada).

Library of Congress Cataloging-in-Publication Data

My body.
    p. cm. -- (World Book's learning ladders)
    Summary: "Introduction to the human body and
how it works using simple text, question and answer
format, illustrations, and photos. Features include
puzzles and games, fun facts, a resource list, and
an index"--Provided by publisher.
    Includes bibliographical references and index.
    ISBN 978-0-7166-7727-7
    1. Body, Human--Juvenile literature.   2. Human
physiology--Juvenile literature.   I. World Book, Inc.
QP37.M9 2008
612--dc22
                        2007018908

World Book's Learning Ladders
Set ISBN: 978-0-7166-7725-3

Printed in China
by Shenzhen Wing King Tong Paper Products Co., Ltd.
Shenzhen, Guangdong
6th printing December 2011

Editor in Chief: Paul A. Kobasa

Supplementary Publications
    Associate Director: Scott Thomas
    Managing Editor: Barbara A. Mayes

Senior Editor: Shawn Brennan

Editor: Dawn Krajcik

Researcher: Cheryl Graham

Manager, Contracts & Compliance
    (Rights & Permissions): Loranne K. Shields

Graphics and Design
    Associate Director: Sandra M. Dyrlund
    Associate Manager, Design: Brenda B. Tropinski
    Associate Manager, Photography: Tom Evans

Production
    Director, Manufacturing and Pre-Press: Carma Fazio
    Manager, Manufacturing: Steven Hueppchen
    Production Technology Manager: Anne Fritzinger
    Proofreader: Emilie Schrage

This edition is an adaptation of the Ladders series
published originally by T&N Children's Publishing, Inc.,
of Minnetonka, Minnesota.

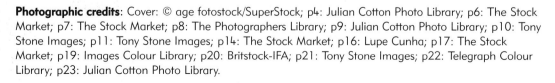

Photographic credits: Cover: © age fotostock/SuperStock; p4: Julian Cotton Photo Library; p6: The Stock
Market; p7: The Stock Market; p8: The Photographers Library; p9: Julian Cotton Photo Library; p10: Tony
Stone Images; p11: Tony Stone Images; p14: The Stock Market; p16: Lupe Cunha; p17: The Stock
Market; p19: Images Colour Library; p20: Britstock-IFA; p21: Tony Stone Images; p22: Telegraph Colour
Library; p23: Julian Cotton Photo Library.

Illustrators: Rhian Nest James, Jon Stuart

What's inside?

This book tells you lots of exciting things about your body. Inside your body, you have soft parts and hard parts that all do special jobs. They work together to help you speak and move, eat and drink, play and sleep!

My body

Your body is amazing! It's made up of a lot of different parts inside a stretchy covering of skin. Girls and boys look different from each other, but their bodies work in the same ways. Can you name the main parts of your body?

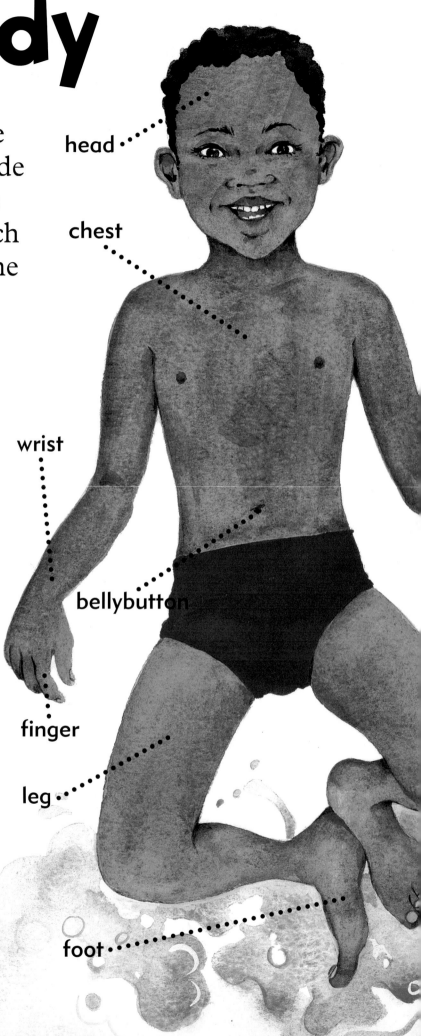

head

chest

wrist

bellybutton

finger

leg

foot

A baby holds his mother's hands while learning how to walk. Soon, he will be able to walk on his own.

hair

hand

neck

arm

shoulder

belly

elbow

It's a fact!

When you're hot, you sweat water through your skin. In one day, you can lose more than a quart of water!

knee

ankle

toe

Bones

Inside your body, you have more than 200 hard bones that are different shapes and sizes. Together they make a big, strong frame, called a skeleton. Try tapping your knee. Can you feel a bone underneath your skin?

Your **skull** is a bony case that protects your brain.

Two rows of curved **ribs** make a large cage around your heart and lungs.

These skaters are rolling quickly along a path. They wear helmets and pads to protect their bones if they fall.

Your **backbone**, or spine, is made up of lots of little bones, like beads on a string.

Three long, straight arm bones join at your **elbow**.

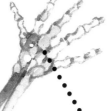

There are more than 25 **hand bones** in your palm, wrist, and fingers.

Your **hip bones** join your legs to the rest of your body.

Your **kneecap** protects the joint where your leg bones meet.

The longest and strongest bone in your body is your top **leg bone**.

Luckily, broken bones are easy to mend. A doctor wraps them in a stiff plaster cast, then they grow together again.

It's a fact!

Lots of animals have bones inside their bodies. Dogs and cats have skeletons, and so do tiny fish!

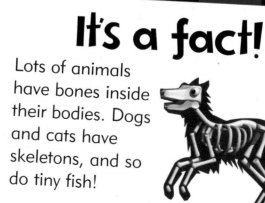

Muscles

Strong muscles under your skin help you bend and stretch your body. You use muscles every time you shake your head, wiggle a toe, or jump up and down. The big picture shows children playing leapfrog. This game uses lots of muscles!

It's a fact!

Exercise makes your muscles stronger. Some people make their muscles so strong that they can lift a car!

Dancing is a really fun way to exercise. Everybody has a good time moving their arms and legs to music!

Bend your back and try to curl up into a round ball.

Pull your knees up toward your head.

Run and jump
over your friend!
Use the muscles
in your arms to
push yourself over.

With lots of practice, your body can do
amazing things. This girl can jump up
high and stretch her legs wide apart.

As you jump,
stretch out your
legs, ready to land
on the ground.

To keep your
head safe, **tuck** it
under your hands.

❤ Inside my body

Your body is packed full of soft parts, called organs, that do extremely important jobs. They help you to breathe, to eat, and even to think. There's also a lot of thick blood inside your body. It carries food and oxygen around, from your head to your toes!

Your **brain** is inside your head. It helps you to think and learn.

When you breathe out underwater, you can see the air come out of your mouth and nose in lots of bubbles!

Every time you breathe in, two spongy bags called **lungs** fill up with air.

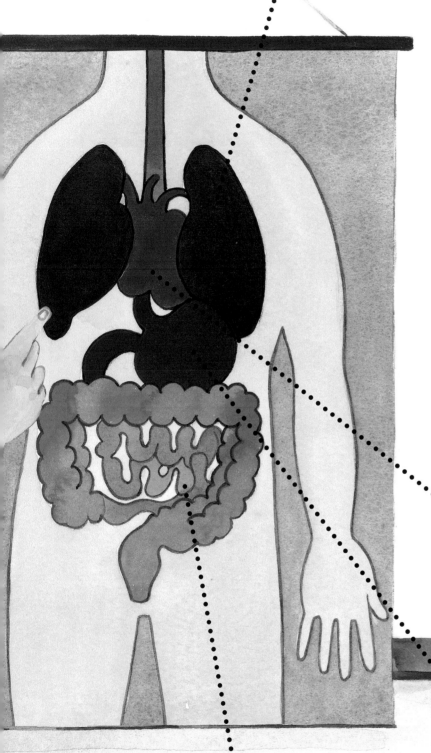

Doctors use a special instrument called a stethoscope to listen to your heartbeat. Your heart sounds like a drum. Thump! Thump!

Your **heart** pumps blood around your body all day and all night.

Your wiggly **gut** soaks up the best bits of food. The rest of it slides to the end and you go to the bathroom!

Your **stomach** churns up all the food you eat into a mushy soup!

Playing in the park

The park is full of children playing different games. They bend and stretch their bodies in all sorts of ways!

12

Which parts of her body does the girl bend to pick up the stick?

Words you know

Here are words that you read earlier in this book. Say them out loud, then find the things in the picture.

knee	elbow	leg
shoulder	chest	arm

My face

Everyone's face is different! Your face is the part of your body that shows people how you feel inside. Crying can mean that you are feeling sad. Smiling shows everyone that you are happy.

Lots of **eyelashes** help stop specks of dirt from getting into your eyes.

When you are happy, your **mouth** curls up into a big smile!

Your **chin** is at the very bottom of your face.

These brothers are identical twins. They were born on the same day and look almost exactly the same as each other.

Your **forehead** may wrinkle when you are mad.

Some people's **cheeks** turn rosy when they are warm.

Your **nose** tells you if a smell is nice or nasty.

Strong, rock-hard **teeth** are for biting and chewing food.

It's a fact!

If you do not cut your hair, it may keep growing until it trails behind you on the ground!

See and hear

All day long, you look at things around you and hear all sorts of sounds. You do it without even trying! The children in the big picture are reading, singing, and playing music. Do you like listening to music?

You can hear soft sounds and loud sounds with your **ears**.

This girl is wearing **glasses** to help her see more clearly.

These children are talking with their hands. They can't hear words so they make special signs that stand for ideas.

You use your **eyes** to look at the world around you.

When you look through a magnifying glass, everything seems really big—even the patterns on a butterfly's wings.

It's easy to **sing** along to the music when you know the words.

As you listen to a tune, try to **clap your hands** in time.

Touch and feel

Does a feather feel soft or hard, smooth or rough? You find out how things feel by touching them. Your fingertips are best for touching but toes are good, too. The big picture shows lots of things you can find on a beach. Can you imagine how they feel?

When you dig your feet into sand, the tiny grains **tickle** between your toes.

Rock is hard and jagged. It feels **rough** against your bare skin.

It's a fact!

Your body hates to be cold. When it gets too cold, your nose and cheeks turn red, or even blue!

Seaweed feels **slimy** when it's wet. It slips through your fingers.

This boy loves his pet dog. He presses his face against the dog's soft, furry coat to give it a big hug.

On a hot day, it feels good to dip your hand in **cool** seawater.

Keep away from a sea urchin or it will sting you with its **prickly** spines!

Taste and Smell

Your tongue does a special job. When you eat, it tells you if your food tastes nice or yucky. Your nose helps, too, by catching smells that float into the air. The smell of fresh popcorn or hot pizza can make you feel really hungry.

Licking ice cream makes your tongue tingle. It feels cold in your mouth but tastes yummy!

Cookies and cakes are baked with lots of sugar to make them taste **sweet**.

Lemons taste so **sour** that eating them makes your face pucker!

Salty chips and peanuts can make you thirsty.

Steaming hot pizza **smells** so good that you can't wait to eat it.

A fresh flower smells lovely. Holding it close to your nose is the best way to sniff its special scent.

Staying well

Your body is a wonderful machine. Just think of all the things it can do. But you must take care of it to stay healthy. You need plenty of exercise, water, fresh food, and sleep. You need to wash each day to keep yourself clean!

Brush your teeth with **toothpaste** to help them stay clean and white.

Fresh fruit is tasty and good for you too. It helps your body grow.

Soap is for washing your skin. You rub it all over—even behind your ears!

If you cut your skin, wear a **bandage** to keep it clean while it mends.

Shampoo gets rid of the dirt in your hair and makes lots of bubbles, too!

Soft, thick **pajamas** keep you warm and cozy when you curl up in bed.

Playing can tire you out. A short nap gives your body a rest, so that you are ready to start all over again.

Fun at the beach

On a hot day, lots of people go to the beach. It's fun to play on the warm sand and splash in the water.

24

Words you know

Here are some words that you read earlier in this book. Say them out loud, then find the things in the picture.

mouth   eyes   nose

teeth   chin   ears

Life Guard

What are some of the sounds the children could be hearing?

25

Did you know?

The facial skeleton is made up of 14 bones and 32 teeth.

Your bellybutton is the place where someone cut a special tube that you needed as you grew in your mother's body. When you were born, the tube was cut and tied, leaving your bellybutton.

Your body is mostly water.

The body has more than 600 muscles!

The heart beats an average of 70 times a minute without rest throughout a person's lifetime.

You blink more than 10,000 times a day.

Your tongue is covered with about 3,000 taste buds!

Puzzles

Close-up!

We've zoomed in on some children you have seen in this book. Can you figure out what they're doing?

Answers on page 32.

Double trouble!

These two pictures are not exactly the same. Can you find the four things that are different in picture b?

Match up!

Match each word on the left with its picture on the right.

1. heart

2. taste

3. ribcage

4. skull

5. skeleton

6. touch

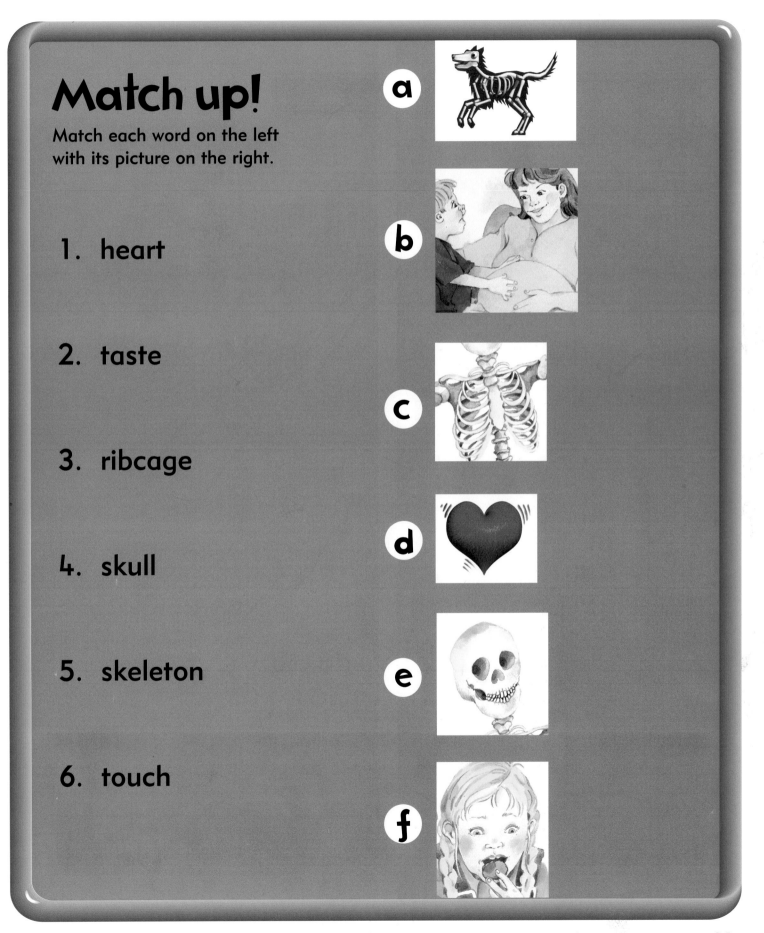

a

b

c

d

e

f

Answers on page 32.

True or false

Can you figure out who is telling the truth? You can turn to the page numbers listed to help you find the answers.

Dogs are the only animals that have bones inside their bodies.
Go to page 7.

3

When you're hot, you sweat water through your skin.
Go to page 5.

1

Some people are so strong that they can lift an airplane.
Go to page 8.

4

If you do not cut your hair, it may grow until it trails on the ground.
Go to page 15.

2

When you feel cold, your nose turns green!
Go to page 18.

5

Answers on page 32.

Find out more

Books

The Amazing Human Body, Leslie Johnstone and Shar Levine (Sterling Publishing, 2006)
Twenty simple science activities help you get better acquainted with your body.

Amazing You: Getting Smart About Your Private Parts, Gail Saltz (Dutton Children's Books, 2005)
This book explains and illustrates the differences between boys' and girls' bodies.

Are You Tough Enough? Paul Mason (Raintree, 2006)
Find out how your body deals with heavy physical exercise and activity.

The Busy Body Book: A Kid's Guide to Fitness, Lizzy Rockwell (Crown Publishers, 2004)
Colorful pictures and diagrams explain how the parts of your body work together and stay healthy when you're running, jumping, bicycling, or otherwise actively moving.

Early Bird Body Systems (Lerner Publications, 2005) 6 volumes
Each book discusses a different system of the body: circulatory, digestive, muscular, nervous, respiratory, and skeletal.

Web sites

BAM! Body and Mind: Your Body, U.S. Centers for Disease Control and Prevention
http://www.bam.gov/sub_yourbody/index.html
"Your Body" is just one of six pages on this government Web site for kids. Here, you'll find news articles, expert advice, stories, and answers to your questions. But don't stop here: visit the other pages, too, all having to do with you and your health.

Kid Info
http://kidinfo.com/Health/Human_Body.html
This search engine links you to many Web sites about the human body, some for kids, some for parents and teachers.

My Body, KidsHealth
http://kidshealth.org/kid/body/mybody_noSW.html
Have fun learning about and caring for your body with such special features as "Kids' Talk," "Recipes," and "The Game Closet."

Human Anatomy Online, MyHealthScore.com
http://www.innerbody.com/htm/body.html
Choose from 10 body systems, such as digestive and skeletal, to get animated pictures of the different body parts belonging to that system.

Your Gross & Cool Body, Discovery Kids
http://yucky.discovery.com/noflash/body/index.html
Follow Wendell the Worm and friends as they explore dandruff, earwax, hiccups, and other weird things about your body.

Answers

Puzzles
from pages 28 and 29

Close-up!
1. washing hair
2. feeling seaweed and water
3. smelling and eating pizza

Double trouble!
In picture b, the boy is bending both his legs, has curly hair, is wearing glasses, and is missing a shoe.

Match up!
1. d
2. f
3. c
4. e
5. a
6. b

True or false
from page 30

1. true
2. true
3. false
4. false
5. false

Index